Makimba's Animal World

Makimba's Animal World

by Bobby L. Jackson

illustrated by Julienne Jones

MULTICULTURAL PUBLICATIONS
AKRON, OHIO

Text copyright ©1994 by Bobby L. Jackson
Illustrations copyright ©1994 by Julienne Jones

All rights reserved. No part of this book may be reproduced
in any form without written permission from the publishers,
except by a reviewer who may quote brief passages to be printed
in a newspaper or magazine.

Published by:
Multicultural Publications
P.O. Box 8001
Akron, Ohio 44320

Printed in the United States of America

1 2 3 4 5 6 7 8 9 10

Library of Congress Catalog Card No: 93-79595

ISBN 0-9634932-9-9 Hardcover

ISBN 0-9634932-8-0 Paperback

Grateful acknowledgement is made to Bill Copeland, Akron
Teachers Credit Union, Irma Petersen, and Bank One
for continued support and encouragement.

For Marleen Shultz-Augustine, my seventh grade Language Arts teacher, who enhanced my self-esteem. You believed in me when others did not.

Āā

Sable (sā′bəl)

Makimba once had a pet sable

Who sat with her down at a table

She fed him a steak

And watched as he ate

Then read her pet sable a fable.

Ăă

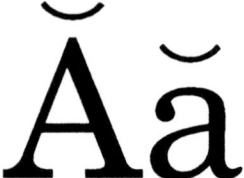

Jackal (Jăkəl)

Makimba once saw a jackal
Who danced and barked with a cackle.

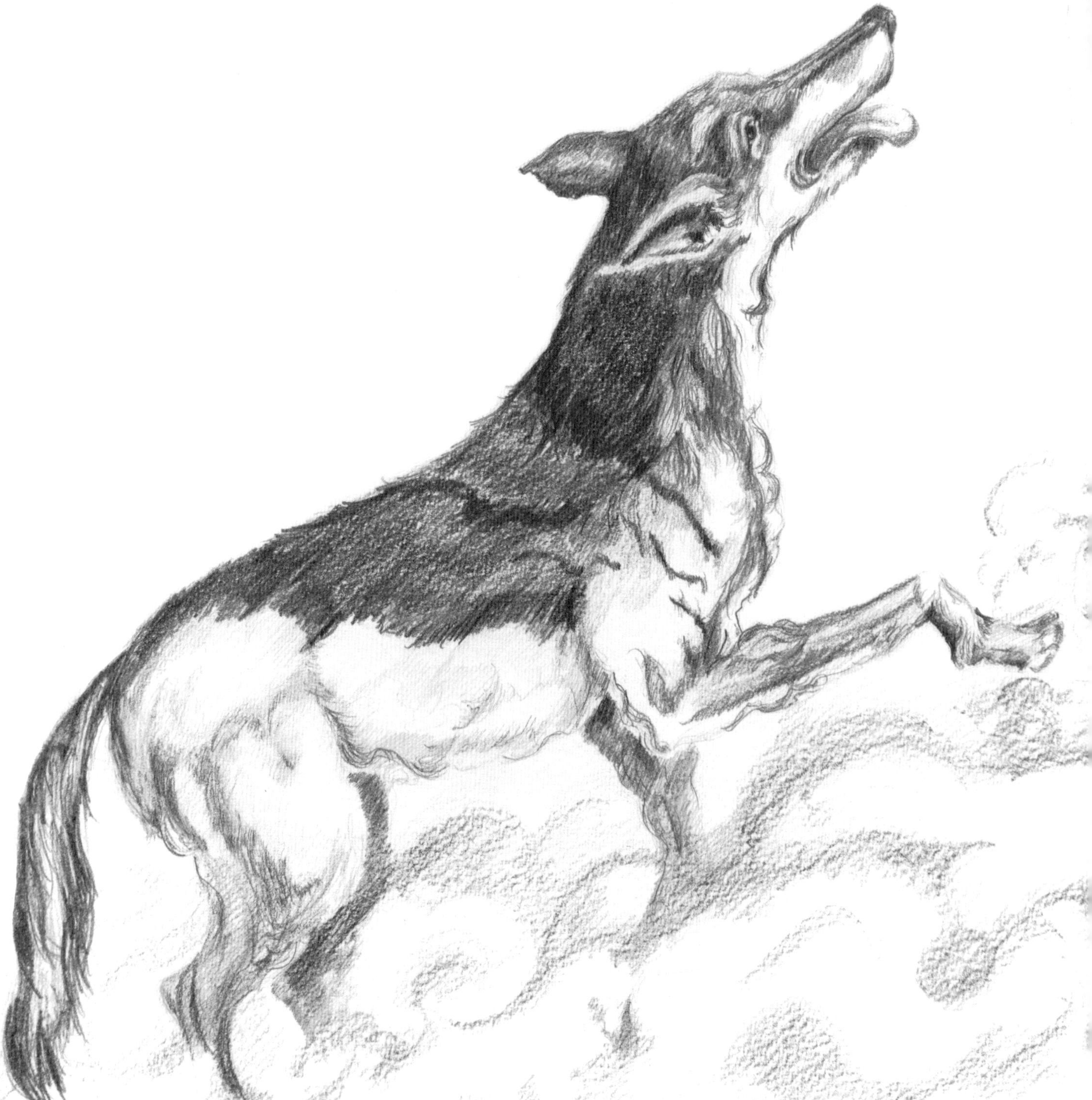

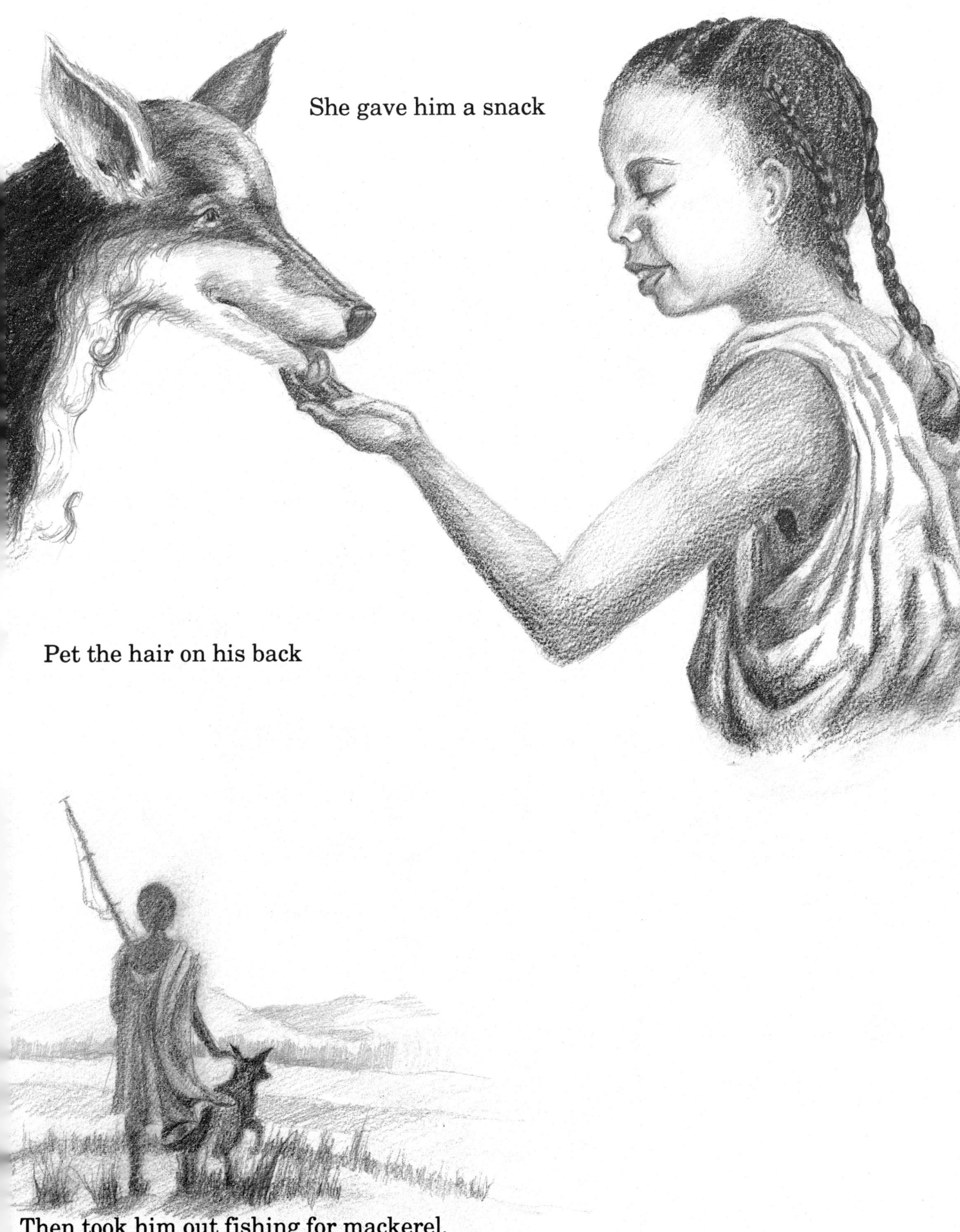

Eē

Hyena (Hī-ē′nə)

Makimba once saw a hyena
Who pranced like a young ballerina.

She howled and laughed
As she walked down a path

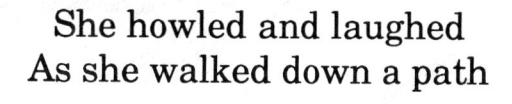

In a brush-covered jungle arena.

Ĕĕ

Leopard (Lǝp'ǝrd)

Makimba saw two spotted leopards
Who spied on two lost lonely shepherds.

It was a bright sunny day

And they wanted to play

So the shepherds made friends with the leopards.

Īī

Rhino (Rī′nō)

Makimba once saw a white rhino
Who must have been an albino.

The thick skinned rhinoceros

Was really preposterous

He thought he was king of the jungle.

Ĭi

Iguana (Ĭ-gwä′nə)

Makimba once saw an iguana
Perched on the back of a llama.

It slid down the hump

And made a loud thump

When it jumped off the back of the llama.

Ōō

Mole (Mōl)

Makimba once saw Minnie Mole
Taking food underground through a hole.

When she peeped in the hole

She saw Minnie Mole

Eating berries and nuts in a bowl.

Ŏŏ

Mongoose (Mŏng go͞os′)

Makimba once saw a mongoose
Its feet were caught in a noose.

She set the beast free.

It climbed up the tree.

Oh... it felt good to be loose!

U u

Kudu (Koo'doo)

Makimba one day saw a Kudu
As he traveled along with the Zulu.

Dinner drums they could hear
As the evening grew near.

The Zulu shared stew with the Kudu.

Ŭŭ

Buffalo (Bŭf′ə-lō)

Makimba was on her way home

The first time she saw buffalo roam.
They were brown and black
And they roamed in a pack.

Except one who was left all alone.

Typography designed by Imagine That Graphic Design

Set in 14 pt. New Century Schoolbook

Edited by April Gordon

Printed by Galley Printing, Inc.

Bound by B & B Bindery

••••••• To order a copy of this book, send **$7.95 (paperback)** or **$12.95 (hardcover)** plus $2.75 shipping and handling (plus .75 for each additional book).
Ohio residents please add 6.25% sales tax.
Discounts are available for wholesalers and retailers.
Please allow 3-4 weeks for delivery

••••••••••••••••••••••••••••••••

Make check or money order payable to:

Multicultural Publications
P.O. Box 8001
Akron, Ohio 44320

Name ....

Address..

City, State, Zip ....

Title of Book: *Makimba's Animal World*

Number of Paperback copies .....x $7.95	☐
Number of Hardcover copies .....x $12.95	☐
Shipping & Handling	☐
Tax...	☐
Total Amount enclosed	☐

Please photocopy this page!